THE HOPPER COLLECTION

Mat Smart

BROADWAY PLAY PUBLISHING INC
New York
www.broadwayplaypublishing.com
info@broadwayplaypublishing.com

I0140964

THE HOPPER COLLECTION
© Copyright 2007 Mat Smart

Cover art design: Huntington Theater Company
First printing: October 2007
I S B N: 978-0-88145-353-9
Book design: Marie Donovan
Word processing: Microsoft Word
Typographic controls: Ventura Publisher
Typeface: Palatino
Printed and bound in the U S A

The play had its first performance on 12 November 2005 and ran until 31 December 2005 at The Magic Theater (Chris Smith, Artistic Director; David Gluck, Managing Director). The cast and creative contributors were:

DANIEL . . . . Andy Murray
MARJORIE . . . . Julia Brothers
EDWARD . . . . Zac Jaffee
SARAH . . . . Anna Bullard

Director . . . . Chris Smith
Set design . . . . Erik Flatmo
Lighting design . . . . Christopher Studley
Costume design . . . . Callie Floor
Sound design . . . . Yvette Janine Jackson
Stage manager . . . . Nicole Dickerson
Production manager . . . . James Mulligan
Technical director . . . . Rachel Hospodar
Casting director . . . . Jessica Heidt
Assistant director . . . . Laley Lippard
Properties . . . . Rebecca Helgeson
Scenic artist . . . . Leticia Samonte
Costume supervisor . . . . Lauren Cohen
Master electrician . . . . Dustin Snyder
Board operator . . . . Nick Shoob
Production assistant . . . . Lisa Ehm

The play opened Wednesday 8 March 2006 at The
Huntington Theater Company, Boston (Nicholas
Martin, Artistic Director; Michael Maso, Managing
Director). The cast and creative contributors were:

DANIEL . . . . Bruce McKenzie
MARJORIE . . . . Leslie Lyles
EDWARD . . . . Brian Leahy
SARAH . . . . Therese Barbato

Director . . . . Daniel Aukin
Set design . . . . Adam Stockhausen
Costume design . . . . Kaye Voyce
Lighting design . . . . Matt Frey
Sound design . . . . Benjamin Emerson
Dramaturg . . . . Ilana M Brownstein
Casting . . . . Alaine Alldaffer
P S M . . . . Stephen M Kaus
S M . . . . Eileen Ryan Kelly
Fights . . . . Robert Walsh
Associate set design . . . . Rachel Nemec
A D . . . . Sarah Martin
Assistant casting . . . . Duncan Stewart
Assistant lighting . . . . Scott Bolman & Nick Houfek
P A . . . . Jessica Besecker

CHARACTERS & SETTING

MARJORIE
DANIEL, *her husband*
EDWARD, *a young man*
SARAH, *a young woman*

A summer evening

The painting is on display downstage and only the back of the canvas should be seen by the audience.

Special thanks: Christine Albright, Rachel Axler, Julia Brothers, Ilana Brownstein, Shirley Fishman, Wes Grantom, Jen Hammaker, Allan Havis, Adam Knight, Barry Levey, Tim J. Lord, Nicky Martin, Jill Matichak, Ruth McKee, Carl Mulert, Mark Routhier, Adele Shank, Brian Slaten, Mark Emerson Smith, Peter Story, Jacob Titus, Lisa Velten, Joe Ward, Ken Weitzman, Chris Wigle, the University of California—San Diego, and my family.

for Ken and Ginger Baldwin

(DANIEL *tries to shadow box like the fighter he once was.*
He has a slight limp. MARJORIE *enters from her side.*
She carries a tray with two glasses of cola.)

DANIEL: I thought I'd come out here and do a little Left
Left Right Right, get the blood pumping, remind you of
what you're missing—who knows, eh? maybe get you
in the mood for a little Left Left Right Right yourself...

MARJORIE: Do one of those...you know, all in a row...

(DANIEL *does an intricate combination.*)

MARJORIE: Oh, bravo. Bravo. Again.

(DANIEL *does it again.*)

MARJORIE: Oh, I like those.

DANIEL: Is it working?

MARJORIE: Not yet, dear.

DANIEL: Give it a minute.
   Before you know it, you'll want to bolt the door and
forget all this nonsense and scream "Daniel! Daniel!
Daniel! For The Love Of God, Daniel!" Should I take
off my shirt?

MARJORIE: Oh, Danny, you're scuffing up the floor.

(DANIEL *speeds up.*)

DANIEL: Grrrrr.

MARJORIE: You know, there are more civilized ways to
express anger.

(DANIEL *stops shadow boxing.*)

DANIEL: Grrrrr.

MARJORIE: Why don't you sit down, have a diet cola, and tell me what's bothering you?

DANIEL: *(Exploding)* You know damn well what is—

MARJORIE: There's no need to raise your voice, Danny. Diet cola?

DANIEL: You're shaking.

(MARJORIE smiles and says nothing. DANIEL takes the glass, but does not drink.)

MARJORIE: Go ahead.

DANIEL: *(With an exaggerated calmness)* Well, dear. I had plans for our anniversary—

MARJORIE: *My.*

DANIEL: *Your* anniversary—plans a long, long time in the making—and I'm rather furious that you've sprung this on me.

MARJORIE: I think you're overreacting.

DANIEL: *(Exploding again)* You haven't let anyone in here to see that damn thing in ten years!

MARJORIE: I think you're overreacting.

DANIEL: *(Checking himself)* I disagree. I think I'm having a rather measured response.

MARJORIE: May I make a request then?

DANIEL: By all means.

MARJORIE: I think you should look at it, see what all the fuss is about, and then maybe you'll have a less belligerent attitude.

DANIEL: No.

MARJORIE: Look at it.

DANIEL: No.

MARJORIE: After all this time—

DANIEL: Grrrrr.

MARJORIE: It would demonstrate such a growth.

(The word stings. DANIEL considers it.)

DANIEL: I...I can't—I couldn't. But know that I have been *working* on it. For the anniversary.

MARJORIE: Well, then. I guess negotiations have failed.

DANIEL: They're strangers! Won't you just tell them to come tomorrow?

MARJORIE: They're on their way, dear.

DANIEL: But why tonight?

MARJORIE: This is how I want to celebrate.

DANIEL: The gift will have to wait until next year then...

MARJORIE: Fine.

DANIEL: Fine.

MARJORIE: Fine.

DANIEL: Fine.

MARJORIE: Fine.

DANIEL: Fine.

MARJORIE: Fine.

DANIEL: Fine, fine, fine! I'm having nothing to do with this mess! I'll be on my side watching the fight.

MARJORIE: Well, I certainly don't want you growling in here.

DANIEL: Grrrrr. Goodnight, dear. *(He starts to exit.)*

MARJORIE: There's cyanide in your glass.
  I put it there for you. I'd like for you to drink it down.

(DANIEL *holds the glass up to the light and then smells it.*)

MARJORIE: And I'd like for you—after you drink it down—to keel over dead as a doornail.

DANIEL: Oh, there's no reason you would've waited this long to do something so uncreative. I thought the Banana Attack was sub-par—but this—this would be hubris.

MARJORIE: Perhaps the creative part is that I'm telling you. And that you'll drink it anyway.

DANIEL: *(Dismissing it again)* Just promise you'll be good tonight and I'll—

MARJORIE: Did you even use that right? "This would be hubris."

DANIEL: Dear!

MARJORIE: Fine! I will try to be good, but nada guarantidos. This isn't Sears! Nunca Guarantidos. Which one is it? Nada or nunca? Isabel!
  Isabel!

DANIEL: You sent her to pick up the boy at the train station.

MARJORIE: Isabel! Mamacita, por favor! *(Pause)* There's cyanide in your glass.
  After you lose consciousness, I will burn your dead body in the fireplace.

DANIEL: We don't have a fireplace, dear.

MARJORIE: The microwave then. One piece at a time.

(DANIEL *holds up the glass.*)

DANIEL: To A Better Time and A Better Way. To All Things Drawn-Out and Excruciating. To Old-Fashioned Unending Agony.

MARJORIE: Oh, shut up and die.

DANIEL: To Big Business and The Dow Jones Industrial Average. To Long, Bitter Toasts. And To The Love Of My Life. Cheers.

(DANIEL *drinks.* MARJORIE *stands in shock for a slight moment, then falls to the floor and pulls on him.*)

MARJORIE: No, dear. I really did this time.
  Please, please, please, forgive me. I really did this time.

DANIEL: Hubris.

MARJORIE: I bribed a lab technician at the—I paid a fortune for it.

DANIEL: "Come one, come all! And see—Hubris On The Floor!"
  There, there. Let The Husband help you up.

MARJORIE: Leave me for the buzzards.

DANIEL: Come now. On three.

(MARJORIE *lies back down*)

MARJORIE: I already see them circling.
  I really thought I did this time. And you were all "bottoms up." That was quite...

DANIEL: Trusting?

MARJORIE: Unexpected. It is all quite unexpected.
(Like a crow) Ca-caa! Ca-caa!

DANIEL: You give me too much credit, dear. Cyanide has the faint smell of almond. The cola smelled of no almond. Only cola.

MARJORIE: So you're alive?

DANIEL: Right here.

MARJORIE: What sound do buzzards make? *(Like a crow)* Ca-caa!

DANIEL: I should think you have it spot on.

MARJORIE: *(Trying to speak as a buzzard would, but sounding more like a parrot)* "Spot-on!" That's more parrot, isn't it? *(The same way)* "Spot-on!"
  I'm lonely.

(MARJORIE tries to pull DANIEL down to the ground.)

DANIEL: My leg.

MARJORIE: I'm lonely, Papacito.

(DANIEL carefully sits on the ground near MARJORIE.)

DANIEL: Hi, there.

MARJORIE: Hello, pookie.

DANIEL: You're looking lovely tonight.

MARJORIE: Thank you. *(Sweetly)* How would you like to be in here yourself one day? Some sort of caveman diorama? I know a taxidermist who... *(Pause)* Why are you still here?

DANIEL: Because you're not very good at killing people.

MARJORIE: No, I mean...why do you...

DANIEL: You keep me on my toes, dear. *(He leans in to kiss MARJORIE.)* You know how I like to be kept on my...

(MARJORIE turns away. An uncomfortable pause)

DANIEL: Do you have everything settled for the evening then?

MARJORIE: I had Isabel make up the two guest rooms. And after she picks up the young Edward at the station, I told her to take the night off. The girl—Sarah— arrives a little bit later so I've arranged a car for her.

DANIEL: You used the telephone and everything?

MARJORIE: It was an adventure. I didn't know we'd upgraded to the buttons and beeps instead of the...the...

(MARJORIE *makes the motion of dialing a rotary telephone.* DANIEL *doesn't laugh.*)

DANIEL: Well, then...goodnight.

MARJORIE: Danny, do we have time? Before they arrive?

DANIEL: No.

MARJORIE: Please.

DANIEL: The sun's not down yet. The light won't—

MARJORIE: For my anniversary.

DANIEL: Oh, for heaven's sake.

(DANIEL *goes to the light switches on his side and turns them off. It is nearly dusk, so the room is still lit without the lights. He turns the lights on, then turns them off.*)

MARJORIE: *(In a younger voice)* What are you doing?

DANIEL: Looking at the light... *(On)*
  And your face... *(Off)*
  Shadows... *(On)*
  Lines... *(Off)*
  And contrast. *(On)* There. Enough of that.

MARJORIE: Keep going.

DANIEL: Time's up.

MARJORIE: Keep going.

(DANIEL *exits.*)

MARJORIE: Ca-caa! Ca-caa!
  "Spot on." *(She goes to her cola and is about to drink it, but sniffs it instead. She reacts strongly to its scent. She takes out a small bottle of cyanide, opens it and smells. She reacts the same way to its scent.)* Oh my. That is hubris, isn't it? Dear, dear lord. Let's find a safe place for you, shall we? Ca-caa! *(She sets the poisoned cola down across the room and then starts to clumsily take off her dress. Underneath she wears an old-fashioned pink two-piece swimsuit. She speaks*

to herself as she changes.) And here, ladies and gentleman, right next to *Summer Evening* by Edward Hopper—we have our newest exhibit—a diorama of what life was like some twenty thousand years ago. Ladies and gentlemen, I give you "The Ice Age." Note the ape-like cranium and limping leg. Marvel at the grunting and unending desire to put a small, hard object where it is not wanted! Look at how the unhappiness of the caveman exudes on everything around him—for indeed, life was much harder back in "The Ice Age". Ca-caa! *(She goes to the light switches on her side and turns them off.)*
   Looking at the light... *(On)*
   And your face... *(Off)*
   Shadows... *(On)*
   Lines... *(Off)*
   And contrast.

(MARJORIE switches the lights back on. DANIEL re-enters with flowers.)

DANIEL: *(As he enters)* I forgot to give you these.

(DANIEL sees MARJORIE in the swimsuit. He drops the flowers.)

MARJORIE: Ladies and Gentlemen, the caveman.

DANIEL: I thought you promised, after that lovely evening last year, after you almost—

MARJORIE: Accidentally.

DANIEL: Took my leg off—that you would never let me see you wearing that thing again.

MARJORIE: I didn't mean for you to see. *(She takes the dress and struggles to put it on.)*

DANIEL: Cover it up. Cover it up. Cover it up. Cover it up.

(MARJORIE finally gets her dress on over the swimsuit.)

MARJORIE: There! Covered! Go back to your cave!

EDWARD: *(From offstage)* Hello? That Isabel lady kinda opened the door and motioned for me "to go right in." I couldn't really tell what she said. But she kinda seemed like she was in a hurry to leave. Um...

MARJORIE: *(Whispering)* Oh, I hate you. I hate you I hate you I hate you. You get the boy settled.

DANIEL: No, no, no. This is your—

MARJORIE: I must put myself together again, thank you very much. *(She exits to her side.)*

EDWARD: But I think she said go right in. Pero mi espanol es un pocito. Mrs Abhalter, my old Spanish teacher, she was kinda going through a divorce and she would maybe get five minutes into the lesson and then just *stop* and say something like "Mis hermanos y mis hermanas, la amor es muerte!"

DANIEL: Grrrrr.

EDWARD: "La amor es muerte!"

DANIEL: In here.

EDWARD: Hey, are these statues like real? *(He cautiously enters. He wears an unmarked baseball cap turned backwards. He carries a backpack and a medium-sized cooler.)* "Hello! I'm Edward. I've come a long way to be here. I'm so glad you answered my letter."

(EDWARD holds his hand out, DANIEL reluctantly shakes it.)

EDWARD: I figured it out on the train ride. When I figure out what to say first—something simple, something I can remember exactly—I find that I am less prone to ramble. See—dut-du-duu— *(He unzips his backpack and takes out his journal. He opens it to a page and points out the writing.)* "Hello! I'm Edward. I've come... a long way to be here. I'm so glad you answered my letter."

(Pause)

DANIEL: *(Calling offstage)* Dear!

EDWARD: Um... *(He nervously puts his journal into his
backpack and as he does, several prescription bottles of pills
fall to the ground.)* Um... *(He quickly puts them back into
his backpack. He zips it up and puts it on his back.)* So...
*(He pulls the cords to his backpack tight. He looks around
the room and sees the painting for the first time. He
immediately turns away and covers his eyes.)* Whoa, whoa,
whoa! That's not it, is it? Is that it, right there? I totally
wasn't like prepared to see it. Darnit! I need to—
I'm going to look away for now. I know it's there.
It knows I'm here. We'll look at each other when we're
both ready...or something. Um...

*(EDWARD mimes zipping his lips, locking them and
throwing away the key. He waits. Long pause)*

DANIEL: We don't let people in here. You have no idea
what kind of exception is being made. And I should
think it was *keen* of you to inscribe the letter to *her*. This
would not be happening if you had written the letter
to me. So this is her thing. She's sprung this on me and
ruined my plans for the evening and... *(Calling offstage)*
Marjorie! *(To EDWARD)* I'm sorry, I'm not supposed to
be in here. I'm watching the fight tonight. Over on *my*
side. But she, as she often does— *(Calling offstage)* Dear!
(To EDWARD) Has disappeared onto *her* side.

   You see—in my opinion—you are far too much of a
liability. Whether your story is true or not—

EDWARD: Oh, I can—

DANIEL: No, no, no. I have no interest in what is true.
There is little that interests me *less* than what is—

*(EDWARD politely takes off his cap. His head is nearly bald
and there is a long scar near one of his ears.)*

DANIEL: Ah...

(Startled, DANIEL *stares at* EDWARD's *head for a few moments.* DANIEL *turns away and continues speaking without looking at* EDWARD *until noted.)*

DANIEL: You're not going to die in here tonight, *are you?*
Because if you do think there is any chance that tonight is going to be...the night—I think you should leave. It would be a very difficult thing for...*her* to see.

EDWARD: There are things that I still need to... *(He turns downstage and looks at the painting for the first time. Long pause)* Wow.
   I understand your hesitation, but for what it's worth, I can tell you that— *(Pointed)* Could you look at me, please?

*(*DANIEL *stares directly at* EDWARD.*)*

EDWARD: I can tell you that it will not be tonight. If you want to speak in more...tangible terms—well, in a way—for me—in *less* tangible terms...the doctors decided to end the...the treatment one month ago. At that time, they gave me the—it's so weird to call it anything, like you're getting a quote on your brakes or something...not that I've ever really gotten a quote on my brakes before...um—so the estimation is three months. However they do that.

*(*DANIEL *moves close to* EDWARD *and looks directly at his scar.)*

EDWARD: Surgery doesn't really work, but I guess they always have to try...um...it's called Grade Four Astrocytoma—it's the sortof Indy Car of brain tumors. And it's kindof super unusual for someone as young as me to get it. I, therefore, get a great amount of joy from likening myself to the other unusual things in the world—like giraffes and porcupines. Seriously. Look at giraffes and porcupines. Ruminate. Ponder. How do they possibly exist? They're so crazy! But there's those long necks eating the leaves off the tall, tall trees and there are those—well, what do porcupines do? They hang from their tails, right? No, that's the...the...

(EDWARD *searches for the word. Pause)*

DANIEL: Possum.

EDWARD: Possums! Yeah. But what the heck do porcupines do? I mean, besides the obvious like *poking.* Do you know?

(DANIEL *shakes his head no.* EDWARD *takes his journal out and quickly writes.)*

EDWARD: "What the heck do porcupines do? Specifically things that are *not* Quill Related." I have a whole section for science questions and another section for—

DANIEL: Okay, then.
  I'll be watching the fight. If I don't see you before you go—I mean, before you leave here—I mean... *(Calling offstage)* Dear! For God's sake! *(To* EDWARD*)* Women... *(Calling offstage)* What is it? Prom night? Is your corsage the wrong color? Did you have to drive all the way back to the flower shop for them to get it right? *(To* EDWARD*)* She should be right in. Good evening. *(He heads off toward his side)*

EDWARD: So you box?

(Pause)

DANIEL: No, I just watch all the...well, all the heavyweight bouts.

EDWARD: But you boxed yourself, didn't you?

DANIEL: Is it my nose that... Well no, nothing serious by any means. Amateur circuits. And quite a while ago. Before I got into the business side of things. *(Of his nose)* Broke it three times.

EDWARD: Eeee. What's that feel like?

(DANIEL *is about to answer, but stops himself*)

DANIEL: Please don't, eh?
  I don't want to know you. Does that land? One Two?

EDWARD: Teach me something. Show me the basics.
Five minutes.

DANIEL: I don't think so.

EDWARD: C'mon, I've never learned how to punch.

DANIEL: I'm going to go now, eh?

(*Again, as* DANIEL *is leaving*)

EDWARD: Because I don't know that much about
boxing, but I know enough to know that the next
heavyweight fight is not for two weeks.
  So I'm curious about two things. One is: the basics of
punching—which I'm sure would take solamente cinco
minutos. And two is: what is it you're really doing over
there—on your "side" —when you say you're watching
the fight?

(*Pause*)

DANIEL: I've been learning how to paint.

EDWARD: Really?

DANIEL: "Really?" Oh, you're a piece of work, kid.
"Could you look at me please?" Twenty years—hell,
ten years ago—I would've *laid you out* for a lot less than
that. When I was in The Board Room, Wearing My Suit,
Talking The Talk—people knew they might need to
duck— "Could you look at me please?" "What is it
you're really doing over there?" No, there is no fight.
All I'm doing is getting some peace and quiet from the
endless hell that is Having A Wife That Doesn't Love
You Anymore But Still Wants To *Talk*. You follow?
(*yelling offstage*) C'mon, dear!

(DANIEL *exits to his side.* EDWARD *stares after him for a few moments. He takes out his journal and quickly writes. He sits and looks at the painting.*)

EDWARD: Why this one? (*He turns to a page in his journal. There is a postcard in a ziplock bag. He carefully holds it up to the painting. He compares the two.*) What were you trying to say to me, Sarah?

(MARJORIE *enters wearing a different dress and holding a book. She looks impeccably sophisticated—as though she could be a different woman from the one that left the room earlier. For several moments, she watches* EDWARD *comparing the postcard to painting.*)

MARJORIE: You must guess. Fantastic prizes to those who guess. (*She sits in a chair and dramatically strikes a pose, holding the unopened book in front of her. She moves back and forth as though she is on a train, holding the pose as she speaks.*)

EDWARD: Um...

MARJORIE: Clue One. (*As a railroad crossing bell*) DING DING DING DING Ding Ding Ding Ding ding ding ding...ding... (*She jumps up, grabs a big Edward Hopper book from a shelf or table and throws it to* EDWARD. *She strikes the pose again.*) Fantastic prizes to those who guess.

(EDWARD, *delighted, starts looking through the book, comparing her to the page.*)

MARJORIE: Three nuns walk into a bar. The first nun orders a water with ice. The second nun orders a water, no ice, but with a slice of lemon. The third—no, no, wait. I messed it up already. Pretend you didn't hear that. Ah-hem. Three nuns walk into a bar. The first nun orders water, no ice.

(EDWARD *holds up the book and points to a picture*)

EDWARD: Is this it?

MARJORIE: Well Ding, ding, ding. Record time. *(She sits next to* EDWARD *and looks at the book with him.)* Don't you love the way he titles things. *Chair Car. Chair Car.* Straight to it. Goose bumps. Forgive my little indulgence here. Danny-boy hates this game. But I love love love it. I have a whole wardrobe.
  Oh! Look, look, look! Before the sun goes down. We don't have much light left. See those windows above? They're diffused of course—so the exposure doesn't damage the canvas as much as it would—but I think it looks so much better in the natural light—rather than the artificial. So much better. The difference really is... I was going to say night and day, but that's sort of... well, let us take a moment to enjoy the last of the natural light on the Hopper.

(Pause as they look downstage)

MARJORIE: It's funny. The light—no matter what you try to do to it to make it less harmful—to diffuse it—it still, very slowly, is ruining the painting. Destroying it. But what is the alternative? To keep it in the dark? Make an airtight and airless case for you—for it— I mean for it... *(Pause)* See there, the light coming in. Some purples maybe. It almost starts to glow. Oh, you picked a good time. These next few minutes are probably the best all day. *(Pause)* I get dozens and dozens of requests and calls—but these people are all so sterile sounding—so academic. And I should only want to share this with those people who *appreciate* it the same way I do...and I can't tell you how much I *appreciated* your letter. I assumed young people today had...well, with the way they dress and talk and the music and guns and how everything is Sex Sex Sex— I had grown to think true love was...
  But then your letter appears...
  So you haven't seen...Sarah in two years?

EDWARD: Two years and a month.

MARJORIE: And is this it? The postcard she sent you? The *Summer Evening* as it were.

(EDWARD *takes the postcard out of the ziplock bag.*)

MARJORIE: Oh, you can leave it in there.

EDWARD: It's better out.

(EDWARD *hands it to her.* MARJORIE *carefully looks at the front, holding the postcard up to the painting.*)

MARJORIE: Loses some of its punch when it's this small, doesn't it? (*Looking at the back, surprised at what she sees*) It's blank—except for your address. How did you know it was her?

EDWARD: She knows I know her handwriting—the way she does the "a" in my name.
    She just left. She didn't tell anyone where she went. Not even her parents. And then one month ago, I get this.
    So I think it's sort of a two-fold thing. One: it's like saying "can you find me?" And Two: why a postcard of this painting? I know she wants me to figure that out—that's why I wrote you the letter about coming here—because if I figure it all out: why she left? What happened? What I did? —then maybe it'll fix things.
    Because this stuff started happening to me after she left. I felt so sad. Like so, so sad. And maybe I somehow triggered it off.
    When I...When I finally found her number after searching and searching—going off the zip code— I called her and said, "I got your postcard. I've got somewhere I'd like you to meet me." And we work out her coming here...and now she'll be here in— (*He looks at his watch*) Oh, crap. (*He goes to his cooler and takes out a Tupperware container and a spoon.*)

MARJORIE: Can I get you something?

EDWARD: I'll need some more ice eventually. To keep this cold. I'm on this super strict organic diet thing. It's supposed to um...prolong the inevitable.

(EDWARD *eats a small spoonful and grimaces. Then huffs it all down at once*)

MARJORIE: Is that cottage cheese?

EDWARD: With three tablespoons of organic flaxseed oil. Yum.

(EDWARD *takes out a water bottle and drinks*)

MARJORIE: All this is making me...would you like a diet cola? or a whiskey perhaps?

EDWARD: Oh, I can't. Only this.

MARJORIE: Do you mind if I...I will be right...oh, wait—here we are... (*She picks up the poisoned cola she set down earlier.*) Let's have a toast, eh? To All The Men In The World Named Edward And The Women Who Love Them. (*She clinks the glass to* EDWARD's *water bottle. She is about to drink the cola when she realizes what she's doing.*) Oh! For god's sake! Hubris On The Floor. I need to be more...

(*She puts the cola back down across the room. She takes some of the flowers and breaks their stems in half. She puts the flowers into the glass. Over the course of the play, the flowers completely wilt and die.*)

MARJORIE: There. Oh, I'm so nervous. Danny made me such a mess and I'm trying so hard not to say anything... "insensitive" to you.
 If you'll excuse me, I just need a little something to wet my whistle if you will. Isabel. Isabel! Mamacita!
 Oh, damn, she is gone, isn't she?
 I will be right—

(EDWARD *offers* MARJORIE *a water bottle.*)

EDWARD: I always have an extra.

MARJORIE: Oh, if that's not vodka, I don't think it'll do the trick.

(EDWARD *opens the bottle*)

EDWARD: You're doing so much for me. Please.

MARJORIE: Don't be silly...unless—perhaps—you have something stronger...

EDWARD: Sorry?

MARJORIE: Something for the pain?

EDWARD: Um...yeah. But I don't think—

MARJORIE: You must share. I am sharing Edward with you, Edward.

EDWARD: Um...

MARJORIE: Just a little something to take the edge off. Not much. A little something.

EDWARD: Hey, I really appreciate all this. But I can't do that.

(MARJORIE *gasps and covers her mouth.*)

MARJORIE: Oh, please forgive me. That was horrible. Here you are—you need that for real pain—and here I am...

(MARJORIE *takes the water and drinks.* EDWARD *drinks his water. They look at the painting.*)

MARJORIE: I met him once. My father was a patron of his. He came to one of our barbecues when he was still alive. I shook his hand. Talked to him for two minutes. He made quite an impression on me...me being young and quite impressionable.

EDWARD: Hey, we didn't. Because you came in and were doing the—

MARJORIE: Right.

EDWARD: "Hello. I'm Edward. I've come a long way to be here. I'm so glad you answered my letter."

(EDWARD *and* MARJORIE *shake hands.*)

MARJORIE: How do you do?

EDWARD: What was his handshake like? Do you remember?

(Pause)

MARJORIE: *(As Hopper)* "'She's like a fish in that lake,' I think your father said. Well, it's nice to meet you."

(MARJORIE *holds her hand out to* EDWARD *and they briskly shake.*)

MARJORIE: "I'm so glad I finally got the opportunity to come out for one of your father's barbecues." It goes on. I remember every word. I torture Danny-boy with it all the time. He probably has the thing memorized by now.

(The sound of loud hammering from DANIEL's *side)*

MARJORIE: So blah blah blah, Father had the connections and after a certain point, Danny-boy had the millions and so...here it is: *Summer Evening.* In the flesh.

(More hammering)

MARJORIE: And it's worth every damn cent—don't you think?

(More hammering)

MARJORIE: What the— *(Calling offstage)* Hey! Cut that racket out, would you!

(More hammering)

MARJORIE: Isn't he awful? I mean, I'm awful. But he is Awful. *(More hammering)* Oh come on, Bob Villa. People are trying to sleep in here.

(DANIEL *enters from his side with a hammer.*)

DANIEL: Dear, I'm almost out of nails. Do you have any on your side?

MARJORIE: What are you doing?

DANIEL: Just boarding up the gift that has to wait until next year.

MARJORIE: Oh, he's still sore about tonight.

DANIEL: It's our anniversary.

MARJORIE: It's mine.

DANIEL: Oh, what do you know?

MARJORIE: *(To* EDWARD*)* He hates surprises. So he bangs things.

DANIEL: Nails, dear?

MARJORIE: I'm out.

DANIEL: Okay, then. I'll have to manage.

EDWARD: How was the fight?

(Pause)

DANIEL: Still on that, eh?

EDWARD: Who won?

DANIEL: Knock out. First round. Real disappointing.

MARJORIE: Sounds like paradise to me.

EDWARD: Five minutes.

DANIEL: Oh, this kid's a real piece of work.

MARJORIE: What five minutes?

EDWARD: C'mon.

DANIEL: I don't think it'd be the best thing for you, eh?

EDWARD: The doctor says physical activity is good.

MARJORIE: What is this talk? He's my guest. Leave him alone.

(Pause)

DANIEL: Well in that case, I suppose I can spare five minutes. I'll be right back. *(He exits.)*

MARJORIE: What is going on?

EDWARD: You'll see.

MARJORIE: Oh, men. Men, men, men and their hammers and secrets and lies. I need someone on my team! Where is this young lady? What is keeping her? I would like to meet her and tell her what an idiot she is.

(MARJORIE goes to the painting. The sound of hammering can be heard again.)

MARJORIE: Just like this idiot here. What is she waiting for? The guy is obviously a hot tamale and blah blah blabbing away. She needs to Nip It In The Bud before it's too late! Grab the knife and say you thought it was a banana! Kill the bastard! Kill 'em! Take matters into your own hands, Woman!

(The hammering stops.)

MARJORIE: Oh, I don't really mean all that.
  I do.
  I don't.
  What do you think of it?

(DANIEL reenters.)

MARJORIE: Go away!

DANIEL: I'm giving the boy a boxing lesson.

MARJORIE: Oh, no no no.

DANIEL: He asked for it.

MARJORIE: Cover your mouth, Edward! His bruteness has become airborne. Don't do this. Some pretty girl will see you boxing—even if it's some amateur league—

DANIEL: Grrrrr.

MARJORIE: And before she knows it she's married to a brute who looks good sweaty with his shirt off and has a kabillion bucks—but he Just Doesn't Quite Do It For Her.

DANIEL: That's enough, thank you!

EDWARD: Whoa, whoa, whoa. It's no big deal. It's just something I've never done before, so I thought it'd be cool. Don't worry about it.

MARJORIE: Oh, fine—but only if you do something for me first. Come here. (She whispers in EDWARD's ear. Unheard:) [Go ask him to look at the painting]

EDWARD: What do you mean?

MARJORIE: Just ask him.

EDWARD: Um...she told me to ask you to look at the painting?

MARJORIE: No no no, don't say that I said it.

DANIEL: Stop it, dear.

MARJORIE: Go ahead.

EDWARD: Um...
  Look at the painting?

DANIEL: No, thank you.

MARJORIE: Look! And then box.

DANIEL: Not now.

MARJORIE: Look, Box—it's easy.

EDWARD: (To DANIEL) You don't look at it?

MARJORIE: He's never looked at it.

DANIEL: Grrrrr.

EDWARD: Why don't you look at it?

DANIEL: No boxing tonight, I guess.

EDWARD: *(To* MARJORIE*)* Oh, please let us box.

MARJORIE: Oh fine, but there is to be no contact! No bruteness please. I will be the referee.

DANIEL: You sure this is alright?

EDWARD: Yeah.

DANIEL: Okay, then. Basic form. Nothing fancy. Stand like this.

*(*DANIEL *stands with his left foot forward and his right foot back.* EDWARD *tries to copy* DANIEL*'s stance.)*

DANIEL: Just like that. Bend the knees a bit. Good. Up on the balls of your feet.

*(*EDWARD *stands on his toes.)*

DANIEL: Not that far. Alright. Center yourself. You centered?

EDWARD: Yeah.

*(*DANIEL *gently presses on* EDWARD*'s chest.* EDWARD *stumbles a bit, but rights himself.)*

MARJORIE: Be careful with him!

DANIEL: Keep yourself centered. Pretend there's a heavy weight between your legs.

*(*MARJORIE *laughs.)*

DANIEL: *(To* MARJORIE*)* Oh, I'm the brute, eh? *(To* EDWARD*)* Good. Now arms up. Like this.

*(*DANIEL *puts his arms up.* EDWARD *copies him.)*

DANIEL: Elbows in. Don't want anyone getting through. Elbows in. Good. Now... One Two. *(He demonstrates with a couple slow punches)* One Two. One Two. That's all boxing is. One Two. This— *(He touches* EDWARD's *left hand.)* Is your shield. And this— *(He touches* EDWARD's *right hand.)* Is your sword. See? *(He demonstrates a few slow punches.)* One Two. One Two. Real easy.

*(*EDWARD *starts doing the same.)*

DANIEL: One Two.

DANIEL & EDWARD: One Two. One Two.

*(*DANIEL *holds his hands up in front of* EDWARD *as targets.)*

EDWARD: *(Speeding up)* One Two. One Two. One Two One Two One Two.

MARJORIE: Slow down!

EDWARD: How fast can you punch?

DANIEL: It's not about how fast you can—

EDWARD: Can you show me?

DANIEL: Oh, I don't know.

EDWARD: C'mon.

*(*DANIEL *throws two simple punches.)*

DANIEL: One two.

EDWARD: You can go faster than that, can't you?

DANIEL: Oh, fine. But only because I'm trying to get the You Know Who in the mood.

*(*DANIEL *throws a few One Two's at a medium speed. Then steadily builds to a frighteningly fast speed.)*

MARJORIE: Oh, bravo! "The Ice Age."

*(*DANIEL *turns his head to look at* MARJORIE. EDWARD *abruptly runs at* DANIEL, *getting himself hit in the face intentionally.* EDWARD *falls in pain.)*

DANIEL: The hell!

MARJORIE: Oh, you monster!

(DANIEL *and* MARJORIE *go to* EDWARD *on the floor.)*

DANIEL: You okay, son?

MARJORIE: *(To* DANIEL*)* Stay away from him.
 You socked him. I saw you do it.

DANIEL: Look at me. Breathe in.

MARJORIE: We need to get him to the hospital.

DANIEL: Please, dear. *(To* EDWARD*)* Can you breathe in
through your nose?

(EDWARD *nods.)*

DANIEL: Hurts like hell, don't it?

(EDWARD *nods.)*

DANIEL: Feels good, don't it?

(EDWARD *nods.)*

MARJORIE: You're all psychos!

EDWARD: Where's the bathroom? I wanna look at it.

DANIEL: Through my living room and on the left.

MARJORIE: I'll take you. Stay away from this brute.

EDWARD: I can go by myself, thank you.

(EDWARD *exits to* DANIEL'*s side.)*

MARJORIE: That's it. Go back to your side, brute!

DANIEL: He did that on purpose.

MARJORIE: You broke the poor boy's nose!

DANIEL: It isn't broken. He'll be fine.

MARJORIE: Oh, you ruin everything you touch!

DANIEL: That boy prodded me before you came in. "What's it like to get hit in the face?" he asked me. He wanted to feel it.

MARJORIE: You socked him on purpose.

DANIEL: I did not!

MARJORIE: I saw your eyes.

DANIEL: Okay fine, Miss—Miss I Thought It Was A Banana!

MARJORIE: I did!

DANIEL: Steak knives do not look anything like bananas!

MARJORIE: Having a limp adds class, dear. I just wish you'd use a cane. Then it would be real distinction.

DANIEL: Not when everyone knows you did it.

MARJORIE: Do they?

DANIEL: Do they! The jokes I get down at the club. You should hear the buzzards.

MARJORIE: Ca-caa!

DANIEL: Damn you! I nearly bled to death! I should think you researched arteries or something.

MARJORIE: "I should think!" "I should think!" You can only think a thing or not think a thing, bastard!

DANIEL: Lower your voice. The boy will hear us.

MARJORIE: Oh, go crawl into your cave!

(The doorbell rings. MARJORIE whispers)

MARJORIE: Oh, of course! You've made me a wreck again and now the young girl is here. *(She starts to exit to her side.)*

DANIEL: Oh, no you don't! You are staying right here and dealing with the mess you've made.

MARJORIE: You're the one socking people.

DANIEL: All the more reason not to leave me alone in here.

(The doorbell rings again.)

DANIEL: Answer the door.

*(*MARJORIE *sinks to the floor near* EDWARD's *backpack.)*

DANIEL: Answer the goddamned door.

MARJORIE: Ca-caa.

DANIEL: Oh, for god's sake.

MARJORIE: *(As a parrot)* "Oh, for god's sake."

DANIEL: You have ten seconds to pull yourself together.

*(*DANIEL *exits to the front door.* MARJORIE *sits up and tries to stand.)*

MARJORIE: "Pull yourself together." "Pull yourself together." *(She sees* EDWARD's *backpack.)* Oh, hello there. *(Calling offstage)* Edward! The young Sarah is here! Edward, are you still in the bathroom? *(She quickly searches through the bag. She finds a prescription pill bottle and looks at the label.)* Oh, yes yes yes. This will put me back together. *(She opens the bottle and shakes out two pills. She puts them in her mouth and swallows.)* Oh, you won't miss two more. *(She tries to shake out two more pills, but accidentally drops the bottle. A handful of pills fall out onto the ground.)* Dammit.

*(*MARJORIE *scrapes the pills into the bottle as fast as she can.* DANIEL *and* SARAH *can be heard from offstage.)*

SARAH: Yeah, I've never had someone standing there with my name on a sign like that.

DANIEL: It was nothing.

SARAH: It was awesome.

✦

DANIEL: Edward stepped into the bathroom for the moment. He'll be back presently.

SARAH: Hey, that bowl was totally in my textbook last year! It's like Thirteenth Century, isn't it?

DANIEL: Twelfth.

SARAH: Shouldn't you have it like in bubble wrap or something?

DANIEL: We believe in the slow deterioration of old, expensive things.

(MARJORIE *finishes putting the pills into the bottle, but pops one last pill into her mouth. She throws the bottle into* EDWARD's *backpack as* DANIEL *and* SARAH *enter.)*

DANIEL: Speaking of which—

MARJORIE: *(Standing up)* Oh, excuse me. Just sprucing up. How do you do, Sarah?

(MARJORIE *and* SARAH *shake hands.)*

SARAH: Hi.

MARJORIE: Apologies for the brute.

(SARAH *sees the painting downstage.)*

SARAH: No way. *(She goes to the painting.)* No way. I didn't believe him, you know? So this is it?

DANIEL: Can't make copies that good.

SARAH: How much is it worth?

DANIEL: I should think you could choose between this and the Dallas Cowboys.

MARJORIE: *(To* DANIEL*)* So sorry that you have to be going, dear.

DANIEL: Back together, eh?

MARJORIE: Oh, I will be any minute now.

(EDWARD *reenters and sees* SARAH. *He stops.*)

SARAH: Hi, Edward.

EDWARD: Um...um... (*He frantically takes his journal out of his bag and turns to a page. He reads it with his head down and starts breathing faster.*) Um... "It is so, so nice to see you, Sarah. I'm excited to hear about what's been going on with you."

SARAH: It's nice to see you.

(EDWARD *looks at her this time*)

EDWARD: "It's so, so nice to see you." Um...

(EDWARD *awkwardly approaches* SARAH *and holds his hand out. She doesn't take it.*)

SARAH: You're not fragile, are you?

EDWARD: Um...what do you mean?

SARAH: You're not going to break, right?

EDWARD: Um...no.

(SARAH *hugs* EDWARD *and holds him tightly.* EDWARD's *hat falls off. As* MARJORIE *watches, she unconsciously grabs* DANIEL's *hand.*)

SARAH: (*Still holding him*) It's nice to see you.

EDWARD: It's nice to see you.

(SARAH *steps away and looks at him, obviously disturbed at his condition.*)

SARAH: Your eyes look the same.

DANIEL: Let's let them alone, dear.

MARJORIE: (*Distant*) Yes. Yes, of course.

EDWARD: Thank you.

(DANIEL *and* MARJORIE, *holding hands, exit to his side.*)

SARAH: They are so weird.

EDWARD: Yeah.

SARAH: It's pretty cool of them to let us come here.

EDWARD: Yeah.

SARAH: So...

EDWARD: So... *(He wipes sweat from his forehead.)*

SARAH: Did you do something to your nose?

(MARJORIE and DANIEL can be heard from offstage.)

MARJORIE: Oh, don't you get fresh with me!

DANIEL: *You* grabbed *me!*

MARJORIE: I thought it was a banana!

DANIEL: Oh, I've heard that one before!

MARJORIE: What am I doing over here?

DANIEL: Shh!

(MARJORIE reenters and crosses to her side.)

MARJORIE: Excuse me. I must lie down. All of the sudden, the walls are— *(She gestures.)* And I have a hankering for some of those...you know those corn chips that are salty and have a little curve to them...Isabel! Mamacita! *(She exits.)*

SARAH: Oh my god.

MARJORIE: *(Offstage, singing)*
I am the Frito Bandito
I love Fritos Corn Chips,
I love 'em, I do.
I want some
I need some
I take 'em from you...
Eee-yai-yai-yai!
Isabel!

SARAH: I hope I'm that crazy when I get old.

EDWARD: Yeah...
  So there it is, huh? Can you imagine having it in your living room—well, whatever kind of room this is? Is it okay if we sit down?

SARAH: Are you alright?

EDWARD: Yeah, I just need to sit down. In general.

(EDWARD *and* SARAH *sit facing the downstage wall.*)

EDWARD: So did someone tell you? Is that why you sent the postcard?

SARAH: Hey, what are you doing?

EDWARD: What?

SARAH: You're not still talking to me like I'm her, are you? It's kinda freaky.

EDWARD: Sorry.

SARAH: I thought we'd only do that when they're around.

EDWARD: Sorry. I didn't mean to.

(*Pause*)

SARAH: I'm gonna get started. (*She takes out her sketchbook and sits down in front of the painting. She starts drawing it. Long pause*) "You're not fragile, are you?" I don't know where I came up with that.

EDWARD: Yeah. I was surprised at how...real it seemed. Even though you're not... You seem really cool and stuff, but you're like totally different than Sarah was. Is.

SARAH: This place is kindof whack, isn't it?

EDWARD: I guess so.
  I didn't mean anything by that.

SARAH: You think they'd mind if I smoke in here?

EDWARD: You probably shouldn't.

SARAH: Or is it going to bother your...brain tumor?

EDWARD: No.

SARAH: They're ultra lights.

EDWARD: I don't care. But I don't think they'd—

SARAH: I'll only smoke one. *(She takes out a cigarette and lights it. She smokes and hums as she draws.)* And I'll blow it this way.

(EDWARD stares at her for several moments, is about to say something, but then stops. He does not look well. He angrily takes out his journal and writes down a few things, then crosses them out. He mouths a few words. Writes and crosses out. He finally reads what he's written.)

EDWARD: "I don't think you should smoke inside. And definitely not by the painting. It's kind of inconsiderate."

SARAH: I'll be finished in four minutes.

(EDWARD angrily writes down a few more words and then scratches them out. He folds his arms across his chest and leans over in pain. After a few moments, he goes to SARAH and takes the cigarette out of her hand.)

SARAH: Hey.

(EDWARD snuffs it out on the floor.)

EDWARD: Look, sorry. But it's rude.

SARAH: Talk about rude—

(EDWARD loses his balance and falls down to one knee. SARAH immediately goes to him.)

SARAH: What do you need? Should I get them?

EDWARD: Only a surfboard.

SARAH: What?

EDWARD: It's high tide, that's all.

(SARAH *leads* EDWARD *back to where he was sitting.*)

EDWARD: No, the floor is better.

(SARAH *helps* EDWARD *to the floor. He curls into the fetal position.*)

SARAH: Do you need a doctor?

EDWARD: Do I need a doctor? (*He laughs.*) I just need a little orange juice.

SARAH: Which way is the kitchen?

(EDWARD *laughs.*)

EDWARD: No, no, no. In my bag.

(SARAH *goes to his bag.*)

EDWARD: The front pocket. There's a clear orange prescription bottle.

(SARAH *looks through the pocket.*)

SARAH: Which one is it?

EDWARD: The one that's orange juice orange.

SARAH: Is this it?

EDWARD: (*To get through the pain, half-singing*)
Take me out to the ballgame.
Take me out to the crowd.

SARAH: Edward, is this it?

EDWARD: Buy me some peanuts and Cracker Jack,
I— (*He takes the bottle from* SARAH *and tries to open it.*)
You know, a lot of people go "Cracker Jacks," but it's really only Cracker Jack...
(*Singing*) I don't care if I never get back!

(SARAH *takes the bottle from* EDWARD *and opens it.*)

SARAH: How many do you need?

(EDWARD *holds up two fingers. He takes the water bottle*
from his bag. SARAH *hands him two pills.*)

EDWARD: And it's root, root, root for the orange juice...
If it don't win it's a shame... (*He takes the pills.*)
For it's one, two, three strikes...
(*Spoken*) C'mon, everyone!
(*Singing*) Three strikes, yer out...
(*Spoken*) C'mon.

EDWARD & SARAH: At the ol' ballgame.

(EDWARD *holds his hand up for a high-five. Gently,*
SARAH *slaps his hand.*)

EDWARD: Go team!

SARAH: What else can I do?

EDWARD: You can stop being alarmed—for I am
"Captain All Right." I am just fine, Sarah. You just pass
the picante sauce and turn on the salsa music. Whoop.
I didn't mean to call you Sarah. Natalie, Natalie,
Natalie, Natalie. (*He curls up again. He bumps his head*
on the floor) Oo.

(*Note: In the stage directions,* NATALIE *will now be referred*
to as NATALIE *instead of* SARAH.)

NATALIE: Ow. Here.

(NATALIE *sits next to him and puts his head on her lap*)

EDWARD: Thanks. That's soft.
     Okay, now. C'mon, orange juice. Get in there. C'mon.
(*As a airline captain*) "We're sorry for the delay, people.
But it looks like we're fifth in line here for the runway."
     You know, you were right. One hundred percent.
I had two tickets for the Super Bowl—why go alone?
     Natalie, Natalie, Natalie, Natalie.
     You are the first girl to ever come up to me like that.
The pretty art student in the coffee shop comes up to
the tired and wet and pathetic young man who's been

looking through the city all night long. Wandering the
streets of that awful zip code from that awful postcard.
Looking and looking, but nobody is Sarah. "Hey, I'm
doing my thesis on Hopper." That was so Awesome.
"Here is one of these pretty girls and she's talking to
me? This actually happens?" A first. I'm big on firsts.
I'm a fan. Superfan. I just got my nose punched in for
the first time, Natalie. I think firsts should punch
something in. A first kiss with a pretty girl. The first
time swimming in the ocean or getting a quote on your
brakes or smoking a—hey, can I have a cigarette?

NATALIE: No.

EDWARD: I feel like smoking a cigarette. I never have
before.

NATALIE: You're in no—

EDWARD: I already have the cancer.

NATALIE: Edward!

EDWARD: Fine. Maybe just to put in my mouth. Not to
light it. So I can be..."cool". (As the captain) "Looks like
we're next in line for take-off, folks. Thank you so much
for your patience. And as always, thank you for using
Orange Juice Airlines." C'mon, Natalie. I'll be James
Dean.

NATALIE: You're not lighting it.

EDWARD: Nope.

(NATALIE *takes out a cigarette and gives it to* EDWARD.
He puts it in his mouth and pretends to smoke.)

EDWARD: You looked so beautiful in the coffee shop.
Smoking your cigarette in the corner. So elegant. You
know...every time I see a beautiful woman, something
inside me sinks so, so low. Can I tell you this? Because
I know—I know it'd be pointless to go up to her and—
what is there to say? There's nothing to say. I see these

beautiful women and I know that I'll never know any of them and...it makes me so, so sad. *(He puts down the cigarette.)* But not as sad as that night on the porch. Looking up at her. Sarah's hands slowly going slow through my hair. We'd been going out for a year and that night I said to her very calmly, "Marry me." I didn't plan it—I didn't even know it was there— "Marry me," I had said. She didn't say anything for a long time and we both were sitting so still—except for her hands...

*(*NATALIE *starts to slowly touch* EDWARD's *head.)*

EDWARD: And so I couldn't figure out if I had really said it, or if I just imagined I had. I said it again. "Marry me, Sarah." She didn't say anything. And I remember thinking, "She must be saying yes with her hands... her hands are going slowly through my hair and that means yes." And then she kissed me...and I fell asleep...and I woke up in the middle of the night and...Sarah wasn't there. She must have left that night, her parents think. But she kissed me and I fell asleep and...

*(*NATALIE *leans down and kisses* EDWARD.)*

EDWARD: "Are your hands saying yes?" "Are your lips saying yes?" "Are you saying yes?"

*(*NATALIE *kisses* EDWARD *again.)*

EDWARD: Please don't.
  She left that night and I don't want to die thinking anything other than that. You're not her. I don't want you to be her.

NATALIE: You know, Edward, I've never gone up to someone like I went up to you. You don't see many cute guys staring at a postcard of a Hopper painting for like an hour straight. People don't look at things like that. And then when you said you were coming here—my

professor has written and called these wackos
before—they always say no. You've given me this.
But that's not why I'm... Here We Are. There's now,
you know?

EDWARD: Um...I...I...

NATALIE: You can let me be me. Or you let me be her.
Either way—

EDWARD: I don't really think I could, you know?
We lied to them...but I can't lie to me.

NATALIE: Then let me be me. Do you feel this?
   This is real.

EDWARD: This postcard is real. That's her "a." Sarah
sent me that painting on that postcard because she
wanted me to know something. I have to figure it out.
I mean, you're my new friend Natalie and you're super
cool and stuff and maybe if things were like totally
different...but things *are* the way they are.

(NATALIE *looks at the painting.*)

NATALIE: The woman looks more like Helen than
anyone real.
   The proportions of the man's body are skewed.
   The door is too tall.
   The shadows are too dark.
   It's too...perfect.
   But I guess I try to do that sometimes...to draw
something more beautiful than it really is. Or was.
(*To* EDWARD) Do you think you might be doing that?

(NATALIE *leans in to kiss* EDWARD. *He moves his head away
and begins to cry.* NATALIE *continues to hold him.*)

EDWARD: I'm sorry.

(*Pause*)

NATALIE: Did Sarah sing?

(EDWARD *shakes his head no.*)

NATALIE: I do. (*She hums a long, sad song. She runs her hands through what remains of* EDWARD'*s hair.*)

(*Eventually, he stops crying and falls asleep. She continues humming.*)

(*After some time,* DANIEL *loudly enters. He carries the hammer and a large, rectangular wood crate with a gift card and bow attached to the top of it.*)

DANIEL: (*Whispering*) Oh—excuse me—

NATALIE: It's okay.

DANIEL: He's not...dead or anything?

NATALIE: No. He's sleeping. He had to take a pain killer.

DANIEL: Good. That's good.

NATALIE: What is that?

DANIEL: Oh, nothing. Do you think I should carry him to his room?

NATALIE: I think he's okay for now.

(NATALIE *lifts up* EDWARD'*s head and moves her jacket or sweater underneath it.* EDWARD *shifts positions and continues to sleep or pretends to sleep.* DANIEL *sees* NATALIE'*s sketchbook on the floor)*

DANIEL: This is yours?

NATALIE: Yeah.

DANIEL: May I?

NATALIE: Um...

DANIEL: Never mind.

NATALIE: I just started it—but you're a big, art dealer tycoon guy. You can look at it if you promise you won't laugh.

DANIEL: I'm not an art dealer tycoon guy.

NATALIE: *(Pointing downstage)* You got that. *(Pointing to the entrance)* And all those statues and bowls. *(Pointing at the crate)* And you got whatever's in there.
Hey—what *is* in there?

DANIEL: I'm afraid it's only for the You Know Who.

NATALIE: C'mon. What if I can get it with rhymes with? Does it rhyme with— *(Like Picasso)* Schmplasso?

DANIEL: No.

NATALIE: Does it rhyme with croquet?

DANIEL: No.

NATALIE: What about Schmedward Schmopper?

(DANIEL smiles and says nothing)

NATALIE: That is so sick. If I had billions of dollars like y'all, I'd—well, first I'd use it to feed the homeless—

DANIEL: *(Overlapping)* I donate to charities.

NATALIE: —and then maybe take my mom on a trip to France and *then* if there was enough leftover, I'd totally get me a Van Gogh or two. A Schmopper. Can you buy like Leonardo's stuff or is that all taken up?

DANIEL: It doesn't quite work like that.

NATALIE: Well, whatever way it works—it's kinda whack how you have this stuff all to yourselves. That's all I'm saying.
   So don't go and look at my little rendering that I just started and judge it, okay?

DANIEL: I'll only look.

NATALIE: I didn't get far.

(DANIEL holds the sketch book and looks at the painting for a long time. He compares the two.)

DANIEL: Oh, yeah. Look at that.

NATALIE: What do you think?

DANIEL: Of yours or his?

NATALIE: Both.

DANIEL: Of his? His is The Worst Thing Ever. Awful. Horrible. Catastrophic.

NATALIE: C'mon.

DANIEL: No no no. I'm serious. I hate it.

NATALIE: Then why'd you get it?

DANIEL: To win over the Battle Ax.

NATALIE: Do you two hate each other or something?

DANIEL: Oh, you're a shy one. *(Pause)* She hates me. I don't hate her. Actually, I love her. Deeply. Profoundly. In ways she doesn't even know yet.

You see, years ago there was a gentleman who set the bar at a rather obnoxiously high place and—how do you say? —*ruined* her perhaps. But I should think— fingers crossed—that this anniversary present will finally put me on level playing ground.

And I thought I was going to have to wait until next year...with you here and all the commotion and such...but seeing the two of you has put her in some sort of Mood. And I must strike while the iron is... *(Pause)* You asked.

(DANIEL starts looking through her sketchbook. NATALIE tries to pretend like she's not watching him, but she does. He looks at two or three sketches.)

NATALIE: Hey, no judging.

DANIEL: No judging. *(He looks at two or three more sketches.)*

NATALIE: What do you think?

(DANIEL *does not answer. He looks at two or three more sketches.*)

DANIEL: Where is this?

NATALIE: At my school.

DANIEL: Uh-huh. *(He flips to another page.)* And this one?

NATALIE: The view from my window.

(DANIEL *flips to another page.*)

DANIEL: Oh, this is wonderful.

NATALIE: Yeah?

DANIEL: Yeah, I bet Marnye would like this.

NATALIE: It's only a million dollars if you want to buy it. *(She laughs.)* Here. You can have it. *(She rips the page out of the sketchbook.)*

DANIEL: Don't. Be careful.

NATALIE: It isn't anything special. I'll even sign it. *(She signs it.)*

DANIEL: No no no. This is Fine Work. This would need to be purchased.

NATALIE: Really, that's okay.

DANIEL: Would a check be all right?

NATALIE: You can just—

(DANIEL *holds up his hand. He fills out a check.*)

DANIEL: What's your last name, Sarah?

(Pause. NATALIE *looks down at her sketch, realizing she's signed her real name.)*

DANIEL: You know, I'll just make it out to Cash.

NATALIE: Hey, maybe there's another one you'd like more.

DANIEL: Oh, no no no.

NATALIE: I...

DANIEL: You're the artist. I am the "tycoon" you say. I like this piece. And I will pay what I should think is a fair price for it.

(DANIEL *takes the drawing from* NATALIE *and gives her the check. She nervously watches to see if he looks at the signature. He doesn't. She then looks at the check and her face drops.*)

NATALIE: Nothing is worth this.

DANIEL: Take the check, young woman. You deserve it.

NATALIE: I wait tables. I make enough to be all right. Money like this makes me nervous.

(DANIEL *puts his hand up to* NATALIE.)

DANIEL: Shh. He's sleeping.

NATALIE: Don't hold up your hand to me. I won't be your good deed for the day.

DANIEL: I'm paying you for your work.

NATALIE: Then give me twenty bucks.

DANIEL: That's ridiculous.

NATALIE: No, this— *(She holds up the check.)* And all this— *(She points around the house)* Is ridiculous. That drawing took me *maybe* four hours. Five bucks an hour. That's twenty. Take this and give me twenty.

(NATALIE *holds the check out to* DANIEL *as* EDWARD *wakes up or pretends to wake up.*)

DANIEL: Oh, sorry to wake you.

EDWARD: It's cool.

DANIEL: Would you like to go to your room?

NATALIE: Take this and give me twenty.

DANIEL: Really. I have no need for the money.

NATALIE: Neither do I!

DANIEL: This is so unnecessary. I was just trying to— oh, fine fine fine. *(He takes out a twenty dollar bill and holds it out to* NATALIE.*)* Four hours at five dollars an hour makes twenty.

*(*NATALIE *takes it and hands* DANIEL *the check.)*

NATALIE: Thank you.

EDWARD: What's the money for?

DANIEL: I was just purchasing one of these fine sketches. *(*DANIEL *holds up* NATALIE*'s sketch.)* So who's Natalie? *(Pause)* You signed it Natalie. Is that your pseudonym?

NATALIE: Um...that's...yeah. That's what I use. For when I sell things.

DANIEL: Well, my two cents—not that it matters— is that you should use something more distinct. Maybe something French.

NATALIE: That's what I thought at first—so...so I was using Amantine for awhile—but then one of my art professors said...she said, why not something Spanish? Like Natalia. Or Natalie. Spanish artists sell very well in...in...um...in many circles—art circles—and so...um... you know how it is.

DANIEL: Well...whatever name you use— *(Looking at the sketch, to* NATALIE*)* You certainly should keep it up. *(To* EDWARD*)* She's quite a catch, son. Don't let her slip away again, eh?

EDWARD: ...Yeah... *(Pause)* Look. Everything I wrote in that letter was true...except that...I never found Sarah. I tried to, but...

DANIEL: Sorry?

EDWARD: This is Natalie. I met her when I was looking for Sarah.

I'm sorry. I should have said something when I first got here.

NATALIE: It was my idea.

EDWARD: No, Natalie, I—

DANIEL: Wait, wait, wait...

So...

So how long have you two known each other then?

EDWARD: Since Thursday.

DANIEL: Oh...I see. Had us fooled, did you?

EDWARD: Please forgive me, I should have—

(DANIEL *holds his hand up to* EDWARD.)

DANIEL: I don't want to hear this, eh? *(Pause)* After seeing the two of you...she grabbed my hand. Came over to my side. Almost kissed me. That's all that matters. It makes no difference who is really who.

EDWARD: Um...

DANIEL: Let's let her be Sarah, shall we? At least for tonight.

EDWARD: But she's not.

DANIEL: This isn't the Boy Scouts. There are no honor badges for courage.

NATALIE: Do you really mean that?

DANIEL: You two aren't old enough to understand this now, but -

(From far offstage, MARJORIE *can be heard singing* I've Got You Under My Skin*)*

MARJORIE: *(Singing)* I've got you under my skin...

DANIEL: Oh, damn. Just don't say a word to her about this. It'll wreck her mood.

EDWARD: But—

DANIEL: No, no, no. I don't care if you're Bonnie and Clyde. Don't go gumming things up for me.

(MARJORIE *enters.*)

MARJORIE: *Spoken)* Launch the nukes! Leave my guests alone!

(*Smoking a cigarette,* MARJORIE *enters with four shiny, plastic top hats. She shoos* DANIEL *away from her side.*)

MARJORIE: Get, get, get! Before I have to call in the F-Eighteens!
   Buenas noches!
   Que es esto? Oh, what, what, what is this? It isn't for me, is it? (*She carefully inspects the crate, doing strange, strung-out-on-pain-killer things. She listens to it with her ear.*) Hello in there. Hello...

DANIEL: Let's go to your side, dear.

MARJORIE: Never! The present—as exciting as it may be—can wait! There are more pressing matters!

DANIEL: We've done nothing but—

MARJORIE: Silence! When I started to see the pink elephants, I realized something horrible. Something treacherous. We have never had a party here. Never, never, never. And we are going to have one right now. Before it's too late! With dancing and music, cigarettes and shiny plastic hats! (MARJORIE *puts a hat on* EDWARD, *then* NATALIE. *She drops one at* DANIEL's *feet. Singing)*
I've got you
deep in the heart of me—
So deep in my heart—
You're really a part of me.
(*Spoken)* What are you waiting for? Baile, por favor!

EDWARD: You want us to dance?

MARJORIE: Why else would I be singing?
(Singing) I've got you
under my skin.

DANIEL: Please, forgive her.

EDWARD: It's okay.

MARJORIE: *(Spoken)* Dance, idiots! While there's music!
While you're still young!
(Singing) I tried so
not to give in

NATALIE: May I?

(EDWARD *smiles.* NATALIE *and him awkwardly dance*)

MARJORIE: I said to myself this affair
will never go so well—
(Spoken) It *is* a party!
(Singing) But why should I try to resist
when darling I know so well
I've got you
under my skin.

(DANIEL *walks up to* MARJORIE *and holds his arm out,
asking her to dance.*)

MARJORIE: Where's your hat, brute?

(*Begrudgingly,* DANIEL *puts on the plastic hat*)

MARJORIE: *(Singing)* I'd sacrifice anything
come what might
for the sake of having you near—

(DANIEL *offers his arm to* MARJORIE *again. She goes to the
painting instead and dances in front of it.*)

MARJORIE: In spite of the wanting voice
that comes in the night—

DANIEL: If it's a party, then let's dance, dear.

(MARJORIE *continues singing and dancing in front of the painting.*)

MARJORIE: And repeats and repeats in my ear—
Don't you know, little fool,
you never can win—
(*Spoken*) Go back to your side! We'll have the party
without you!

DANIEL: But I have something planned for us.

MARJORIE: You're ruining the romantic evening for
these two birds!

(EDWARD *and* NATALIE *stop dancing.*)

DANIEL: And us!

MARJORIE: Oh, shut up and die already!

EDWARD: Stop doing this to each other! Please.
(*To* MARJORIE) You think we're two little birds here?
You think we're so wonderful and beautiful?

DANIEL: Edward, you've had yourself a busy day.
What if I show you to your room?

NATALIE: (*To* MARJORIE, *speaking of* DANIEL) He loves
you!

DANIEL: That's enough, thank you!

NATALIE: He told me that he loves you!

MARJORIE: This is a party. Parties are for dancing and
smoking and drinking and being young and being in
love and Having Everything In Front Of You Like
You'll Never Have It Again In Your Life! Dance, you
idiots! Enjoy the evening! Before you're old, miserable
buzzards—angry that things didn't go your way.
(*Singing*) Use your mentality
wake up to reality—

DANIEL: (*Tenderly*) There, there, dear.

(MARJORIE *tries to push* DANIEL *away, but they end up half-dancing as* MARJORIE *holds onto him.*)

MARJORIE: *(Half-singing)* But each time I do
just the thought of you
makes me stop
before I begin...
Yes, I've got you
under my...
(Spoken) Will you tell these idiots to dance, Danny?
  Tell them to dance while there's still time.

(Pause)

DANIEL: How about we get everyone settled for the evening? I'm afraid we're not used to entertaining here and we're a bit worn out.

MARJORIE: *(Weakly)* We can't forget the ice.

DANIEL: What's that, dear?

MARJORIE: He said he would need more ice for his cooler.

EDWARD: It can wait until the morning.

MARJORIE: Don't be foolish. We're going to get at least one thing right tonight. Show him the ice, Danny. *(Pause)* Show him to the damn ice!

DANIEL: Of course, dear. Of course. *(To* EDWARD*)* Why don't you come with me?

EDWARD: Thank you. I would've forgotten.

(EDWARD *takes his cooler and* DANIEL *leads him off to his side.*)

DANIEL: Right this way.

(EDWARD *and* DANIEL *exit. As* MARJORIE *speaks, she goes to* EDWARD's *backpack and takes out the clear orange prescription bottle.*)

MARJORIE: Three nuns walk into a bar. The first nun orders a water with ice.

NATALIE: What are you doing?

MARJORIE: The second nun orders a water, no ice, but with a slice of lemon. The third orders a Maker's Mark Manhattan with a wedge of orange—a wedge, mind you, not a slice.

(MARJORIE *has taken out two pills and is about to swallow them.* NATALIE *goes to* MARJORIE *and gently puts her hands over* MARJORIE's.)

MARJORIE: It's just a little something to put me back together—he told me earlier that I could help myself...

(NATALIE *takes the pills out of* MARJORIE's *hands and puts them back into the bottle.*)

MARJORIE: Am I the most horrible person you've ever met?

NATALIE: No.

(NATALIE *puts the bottle into* EDWARD's *backpack and zips it up.*)

MARJORIE: All this time with no one on my side— and finally... Here You Are. Another woman. Another set of tubes. And what kind of role model am I being?

(*Pause*)

NATALIE: What...what happened?

MARJORIE: Really, dear, it's much too late in the evening to—

NATALIE: What happened between you two?

MARJORIE: I'm having a cigarette. Since other substances are being prohibited.

(MARJORIE *takes a pack of cigarettes from her purse.*
She offers one to NATALIE. *She takes one.* MARJORIE *takes*
out a book of matches.)

MARJORIE: What happened between the two us?
(*She strikes a match and watches it. She holds it until*
it burns out.) That's what.

(MARJORIE *strikes another match and lights* NATALIE's
cigarette. She then lights her own. They smoke.)

MARJORIE: There was a time when I loved him. At the
beginning. And there was a time when he loved me—
I mean really loved me—he only thinks he loves me
now—but really, I'm just another project—another
challenge—another Thing He Can't Do. And I should
think—oh, I hate using that idiotic phrase, I get it from
him—grrrrr...I should think that *that* is what I *admire*
about him most: he is truly, wonderfully, thoroughly—
a brute. A brute's brute. He doesn't give up. Never—
in my life—have I ever seen him give up on anything.
He wasn't a serious boxer. He wasn't very good at
all—I mean, for god's sake, look at that nose...but he
could be in that ring—so bloody he couldn't see—
and He Would Not Go Down. Not ever. Not once.
Oh, he'd lose by points, technicalities—but he was
never knocked down. Unfortunately for him, pure
brutes don't make very good boxers and they certainly
don't make good lovers...however, they do make the
best businessmen.
　　Oh, for Christ's sake—listen to me—I should think
I'm going to ask you to paint my toenails next. Excuse
me while I puke my guts out.

NATALIE: The first time I saw Edward...um...

MARJORIE: Oh, wonderful. My stomach is churning
already.

NATALIE: He was—we were—at a coffee shop. I was
sitting in the corner—at the table I usually sit. He came

in and ordered a hot chocolate that he never even
drank. He would only sort of sniff it sometimes. And
he was kinda wet—it had been raining that day—
and he sat down alone and...he looked so sad. And I...
I watched him for about an hour like that. Wet and sad
and...and so I went up to him to...introduce myself—
I'd never done that before, just gone up to some guy
I didn't know, but I just *had* to. I guess...because...I...

(DANIEL *and* EDWARD *reenter and* NATALIE *stops talking.*
MARJORIE *holds her hand up to them*)

MARJORIE: You what, dear?

NATALIE: I guess I had somehow—over that
hour—fallen in love with him.

(*Pause.* EDWARD *stares at* NATALIE.)

DANIEL: Well, Marjorie, we got the boy plenty of ice.
(*To* EDWARD) And I should think you've had quite a
long day, eh?

(EDWARD *continues to stare at* NATALIE.)

DANIEL: Would you like me to show you to your room,
son?

(EDWARD *turns and stares at the painting.*)

MARJORIE: And ah...you know, feel free to *bunk*
together. Don't be shy about it. We don't mind at all.

(EDWARD *continues to stare at the painting.*)

DANIEL: Son?

EDWARD: They're both on the porch together.
  He's asking the girl he loves to marry him.
  But she...she's not ready for this. She wants to tell
him that she loves him, but that she's not ready to be
stuck in this town on this porch with some boy who
doesn't know what it's like to...to have the same thing
happening to him. To be scared by how sure someone

can be. To learn what it feels like to say no to them.
Or to say yes.

To say maybe. *(To* NATALIE*)* Thank you for coming
up to me in the coffee shop. I wanted to talk to you—
I saw you as soon as I came in...in the corner with your
cigarette and your sketch book...

You know, I always take a walk before I go to sleep.
The fresh air is good for me.

NATALIE: Are you feeling well enough?

EDWARD: Yes.

DANIEL: Well then, take your time. The two guest
rooms are made up. When you come back in, just
follow the main hallway straight around. They're
on the right.

EDWARD: Thank you.

*(*NATALIE *and* EDWARD *exit.)*

MARJORIE: Well, the birds are certainly chirping tonight.
Aren't they?

DANIEL: Ca-caa. Ca-caa.

*(*DANIEL *picks up the hammer and holds it out to* MARJORIE*.)*

MARJORIE: Watch where you point that thing, brute.

DANIEL: Why don't you open it?

MARJORIE: You're going to trust me with that?

DANIEL: I'm taking my chances.

MARJORIE: Well, then. *(She takes the hammer and walks to
the crate.)* A card and everything. *(She opens the card.)*
"Happy Anniversary, Marnye. I've been working on
this for quite a few years. Hope you like it. Hugs,
Danny-boy." Isn't that sweet?

DANIEL: Hugs!

MARJORIE: Kisses! Well. Here we go.

*(MARJORIE awkwardly goes to work at opening the crate.
After much deliberation, she gets the top of it off. She eagerly
looks inside and very carefully pulls out a canvas so that its
back faces downstage. Her face turns from anticipation to
complete confusion—then horror. DANIEL beams. She
carefully puts the painting down, resting it against the crate.
She goes to the original painting on the downstage wall.
She inspects the bottom right corner of it closely. She goes
back to the new canvas and inspects its bottom right corner.
She picks up the hammer and charges DANIEL.)*

MARJORIE: Don't you fuck with me! Not about this!
Which one is which? Are they both fakes?

DANIEL: Whatever do you mean, dear?

MARJORIE: *(Pointing at the downstage painting)* Has this
been a fake the whole time?

*(DANIEL laughs. MARJORIE holds the hammer like a baseball
bat.)*

MARJORIE: You already dodged one bullet tonight.
This one won't miss.

DANIEL: Use your nose.

MARJORIE: I will knock your head off!

DANIEL: Smell them.

MARJORIE: What?

DANIEL: Smell them both.

*(MARJORIE goes to the downstage painting and smells the
canvas.)*

MARJORIE: Snf. Snf. *(She goes to the new canvas and smells
it.)* Snf. *(She coughs.)* What?

DANIEL: It didn't get smeared, did it? Putting it in the
crate while the oil wasn't quite yet dry? *(He walks over
to the new canvas.)* Can't tell the difference, can you?
I even got his signature down to a science, didn't I?

(MARJORIE *drops the hammer on the ground in shock.*)

DANIEL: Oh, that face is priceless, dear. I've waited so long for this and it is *absolutely priceless.*

MARJORIE: I've never seen you look at it. You said you never have.

(DANIEL *walks downstage, feigning intense ceremony and then abruptly and sarcastically looks at the canvas. Very deliberately, he looks at the whole thing.*)

DANIEL: Why don't you go over to my side? Into my study. Do you remember how to get there? I've put out some things for you to see. They should clear up any doubt you may have.

MARJORIE: Who are you?

DANIEL: Why don't you go on and look?

(MARJORIE *slowly exits.* DANIEL *moves the crate into position. He goes to the light switches and turns off all the lights except for the single light that is directly above the center of the room. He turns it off. He turns it on. He then goes to the brown bag and takes out a gray t-shirt, white shoes and some hair wax. He takes off his dress shirt and puts on the gray T-shirt. He takes off his own shoes and puts on the others. He takes the hair wax, smears a bit on his hands and then goes downstage to the painting. He styles his hair accordingly. He hears* MARJORIE *coming back and quickly goes to the far corner of the room where he can't be seen. She reenters.*)

MARJORIE: How many are there?

DANIEL: Seventy-three.

MARJORIE: How long...have you...

DANIEL: The first several or so took me about a year each. And they were quite horrible, as you could see. But I slowly started making improvements. Figuring things out.

The most helpful thing, however—whenever you were away—would be to come in here and sit and stare and stare and stare at that awful thing.

To do one now only takes me a week or two. But I'd always mess up one or two details—minor things. The collarbone, for example, is especially difficult. Yet I should think this last one here—the gift—I should think I finally got it spot on.

Are you still wearing the swimsuit?

MARJORIE: Yes.

DANIEL: Then take off your dress.
Take it off. Take off your dress.

(MARJORIE *does. She is in only the pink suit and her shoes.*)

DANIEL: Leave the shoes on.

MARJORIE: What is this?

DANIEL: The shoes?

MARJORIE: They're on.

(DANIEL *steps out to where she can see him.*)

MARJORIE: What is that you're...

(MARJORIE *gasps. After several moments,* DANIEL *quickly walks toward her. He speaks in the voice that is not his own.*)

DANIEL: Is the bathroom through here? Do you know, young lady?

MARJORIE: A little deeper than that.

(DANIEL *lowers his voice a little.*)

DANIEL: Is the bathroom through here? *(In his own voice)* That right?

MARJORIE: Yes.

DANIEL: Tell me if I do anything wrong. *(In the voice)* Is the bathroom through here? Do you know, young lady?

MARJORIE: *(As a younger version of herself)* Um...yes, sir. It's the first door on the left after our living room.

DANIEL: Oh, so you're the daughter? Your father wanted to introduce us earlier, but I guess you were...

MARJORIE: Swimming?

DANIEL: "She's like a fish in that lake," I think your father said. Well, it's nice to meet you.

(He holds out his hand. She shyly shakes it.)

DANIEL: I'm so glad I finally got the opportunity to come out for one of your father's barbecues.

MARJORIE: My father is a great admirer of your work, Mister Hopper.

DANIEL: And I am a great admirer of your father's generosity.
   Say, you better cover up, it must've dropped fifteen, twenty degrees when the sun set. *(He crosses past her, but then stops.)* Wait...wait...could you do me a favor? It'll take two minutes of your time.

MARJORIE: Yes?

DANIEL: Could you stand over there? Right by the porch ledge? Kinda lean against it?

(She leans against the crate.)

MARJORIE: Here?

DANIEL: A bit over.

(She does.)

DANIEL: Swell. *(He moves near her.)* Let's see. *(He rests his arms behind himself.)* Hm. Say, could you put your arms like this?

(She does.)

DANIEL: Swell. Look down a little, could you? Well, no. Chin up, but sort of bring your eyes down. Look down to about where that crack is on the...

(She does.)

DANIEL: There. Swell. Let's see. *(He crosses his arm and leans against the ledge. To himself)* No.

(He changes his arm position. They are now in the exact same positions as in the painting.)

DANIEL: Hm. There. That's it. That's it right there. *(Pause)* What are you? Seventeen? Eighteen?

MARJORIE: *(Lying)* Eighteen.

DANIEL: Say—is the button for that wonderful light inside the door there?

MARJORIE: Yes.

DANIEL: No, don't move. I only need to do one more thing.

(He goes to the light switch. He turns it off. It is completely dark. Beat. Turns it on. Beat. Turns it off)

MARJORIE: What are you doing?

DANIEL: Looking at the light... *(On)*
  And your face... *(Off)*
  Shadows... *(On)*
  Lines... *(Off)*
  And contrast. *(He switches it on again.)* My, my, my— you make me wish I was a younger man standing on this porch with you. But I'm old and married and can only imagine to be anything but. *(Pause)* Excuse me for that.
  First door on the left? After the living room?

(She nods)

DANIEL: Thank you. *(He leaves. Long pause. In* DANIEL's *own voice)* That's that.

MARJORIE: *(In her normal voice)* Turn it off, Danny.
Turn it off again and come here.

*(He turns off the light. The sound of her kissing him.
They slowly lower themselves to the floor.)*

MARJORIE: Oh, yes.

DANIEL: My love.

MARJORIE: Oh, your hands. I love your hands.
Oh, Edward.

(He can be heard moving away.)

MARJORIE: Where are you going?

DANIEL: Can you please not call me that?

MARJORIE: Come back.

DANIEL: Will you try?

MARJORIE: Anything you say. Come back here.

(DANIEL lowers himself again.)

MARJORIE: Breathe on my ear. I love it when you
breathe on my—

(He does. This continues for several moments.)

MARJORIE: Oh. Oh, yes. Oh, Edward.

(He immediately stands up and goes across the room)

MARJORIE: No no no no no. It won't happen again.
It slipped. It—

(He turns on all the lights.)

MARJORIE: Turn off the lights.

DANIEL: *(Of the replica)* I did this!

MARJORIE: Turn off the lights!

DANIEL: I want the lights on! I want you to kiss me and
call me Daniel. Can you do that?

MARJORIE: Please let me have this one night with him. Isn't that part of the gift?

DANIEL: I thought it could be...

MARJORIE: Can't you give me one night!

DANIEL: I thought I could...oh, what the hell am I doing? This is not a shirt I would ever wear! These are not my shoes!

What the hell am I doing?

Those kids couldn't go through with the lie and I don't think I can either.

That is not Sarah. Sarah's gone. The boy tried to find her, but he couldn't. That's Natalie.

MARJORIE: You're making things up now. You're ruining your wonderful gift.

DANIEL: *(Of the replica)* It's not real! It's still not mine. It's his. Everything in this house belongs to him! Because years and years ago—this man—this artist— talked to you for two minutes and turned a light off and on and off and on and put you in some painting—that I paid half my fortune to get for you and— *(He goes to the original painting.)* And I hate it! And not just because you don't love me. I hate it because you've wasted your life comparing everything to those two worthless minutes. And you're still up there! You are still up there and it doesn't matter how much I need you here. Here! Here! Here! Here! I need you to step out of that goddamned thing and finally see *us* and love *us*... Will you, Marjorie? Will you? Will you? Will you? Will you? Will you?

(MARJORIE still can't face him. She goes to the original painting. Pause. DANIEL goes to the poisoned glass of cola. He takes out the dead flowers.)

DANIEL: I guess cyanide's not great for flowers either, eh?

I wish I didn't love you, but I do—I can't help it.
(DANIEL *holds the glass up to* MARJORIE.) To A Better
Time and A Better Way. To All Things Drawn-Out
and Excruciating. To Old-Fashioned Unending Agony.
To Big Business and The Dow Jones Industrial Average.
To Long, Bitter Toasts. And To The Love Of My Life.
Cheers.

(DANIEL *raises the glass.* MARJORIE *pulls the original
painting off of the wall and punches her hand through the
canvas.* DANIEL *does not drink from the glass. He watches*
MARJORIE. *She rips the canvas the length of the painting.
She raises it and smashes it on the ground, over and over,
trying to break the frame.*)

(*When she is finished thoroughly destroying it, she stands
and faces* DANIEL. *He faces her.* DANIEL *lowers the glass
and does not drink from it. They stand there looking at each
other as if for the first time.*)

(*Blackout*)

END OF PLAY

www.ingramcontent.com/pod-product-compliance
Lightning Source LLC
Chambersburg PA
CBHW052222090426

42741CB00010B/2636